"Once again Derek Prince has demonstrated his God-given ability to state important issues with great clarity and discernment. In these days of increasing apostasy and of downgrading of Scripture, it is refreshing to have such a clear exposition on the vital issue of judging. Through the author, the Holy Spirit has given us great clarity on this matter, for instance, in relating judgment to authority. The issue of judging confronts us as Christians almost on a daily basis. Hence I commend *Judging: When? Why? How?* to all who are seeking the face of God and thank Him for the clear expository teaching that it contains. As usual, Derek Prince has put complex matters into a simple, direct teaching, which every Christian can understand. This is one of his great gifts from the Lord."

—Bill Subritzky
Evangelist and Author, New Zealand

JUDGING

WHEN?

WHY?

HOW?

JUDGING

WHEN?
WHY?
HOW?

DEREK PRINCE

w

WHITAKER
HOUSE

JUDGING: WHEN? WHY? HOW?

Derek Prince Ministries–International
P.O. Box 19501
Charlotte, NC 28219-9501

ISBN: 0-88368-695-3
Printed in the United States.
© 2001 by Derek Prince Ministries–International

Whitaker House
30 Hunt Valley Circle
New Kensington, PA 15068

Library of Congress Cataloging-in-Publication Data

Prince, Derek.
  Judging : when? why? how? / by Derek Prince.
      p. cm.
  ISBN 0-88368-695-3 (pbk.)
  1. Judgment—Biblical teaching. I. Title.
BS2417.J83 P75 2001
262'.8—dc21   2001004320

1 2 3 4 5 6 7 8 9 10 11 12 / 09 08 07 06 05 04 03 02 01

CONTENTS

INTRODUCTION

Judging is one of the most difficult subjects in the Bible to grasp, but it is also very important. It is a subject on which there is tremendous ignorance among Christians at large—and consequently tremendous disobedience. It costs us all dearly. Multitudes of Christians, partly through ignorance and partly through disobedience, often act contrary to Scripture in the ways they do or do not judge.

There is an apparent paradox in the statements of Scripture, primarily in the New Testament, about whether or not we are to judge. A number of passages say that we are not to judge and just about as many say that we are to judge. Which are we to follow? We will look at some of the Scripture passages on both sides. Then I will offer a principle by which we can understand in any given situation whether we are to judge or not to judge.

1
SCRIPTURES AGAINST JUDGING

First let's look at some of the Scriptures against judging. In the Sermon on the Mount Jesus said,

[1] Judge not, that you be not judged.

[2] For with what judgment you judge, you will be judged; and with the measure you use, it will be measured back to you.

[3] And why do you look at the speck in your brother's eye, but do not consider the plank in your own eye?

[4] Or how can you say to your brother, "Let me remove the speck from your eye"; and look, a plank is in your own eye?

[5] Hypocrite! First remove the plank from your own eye; and then you will see clearly

*to remove the speck from your brother's
eye.* (Matthew 7:1–5)

Here, Jesus was saying very emphatically,
"Do not judge. If you do, the judgment you
use will come back to you." Judging will evoke
this, I believe, from two sources: human and
divine. In the long run, people judge you as
you judge them. In addition, God will judge
you in accordance with the way you have
judged people.

> [1] *Therefore you are inexcusable, O man,
> whoever you are who judge, for in what-
> ever you judge another you condemn your-
> self; for you who judge practice the same
> things.*
>
> [2] *But we know that the judgment of God is
> according to truth against those who prac-
> tice such things.*
>
> [3] *And do you think this, O man, you who
> judge those practicing such things, and
> doing the same, that you will escape the
> judgment of God?* (Romans 2:1–3)

Romans 2 addresses essentially religious
people. The Jews are the example in this case,
but this passage applies in many ways to
most religious people. Have you ever noticed
that religious people often think that because
they know what is right and can prove others
wrong, that proves themselves to be right?

But, this is not so! In fact, the people who are always judging others are usually wrong themselves.

> [1] *Receive one who is weak in the faith, but not to disputes over doubtful things.*
>
> [2] *For one believes he may eat all things, but he who is weak eats only vegetables.*
>
> [3] *Let not him who eats despise him who does not eat, and let not him who does not eat judge him who eats: for God has received him.*
>
> [4] *Who are you to judge another's servant? To his own master he stands or falls. Indeed, he will be made to stand, for God is able to make him stand.*
>
> (Romans 14:1–4)

A little further on in the same chapter, it says,

> [10] *But why do you judge your brother? Or why do you show contempt for your brother? For we shall all stand before the judgment seat of Christ.*
>
> [11] *For it is written: "As I live, says the Lord, Every knee shall bow to Me, And every tongue shall confess to God."*
>
> [12] *So then each of us shall give account of himself to God.*

JUDGING: WHEN? WHY? HOW?

¹³ Therefore let us not judge one another anymore, but rather resolve this, not to put a stumbling block or a cause to fall in our brother's way. (Romans 14:10–13)

Paul wrote this to the Corinthians:

¹ Let a man so consider us, as servants of Christ and stewards of the mysteries of God.

² Moreover it is required in stewards that one be found faithful.

³ But with me it is a very small thing that I should be judged by you or by a human court. In fact, I do not even judge myself.

⁴ For I know nothing against myself, yet am I not justified by this.
(1 Corinthians 4:1–4)

That's a remarkable statement! Paul was saying, "I am not conscious of anything against me; I'm not aware of anything I've done wrong." But that did not justify him. It did not prove him righteous!

⁴ He who judges me is the Lord.

⁵ Therefore judge nothing before the time, until the Lord comes, who will both bring to light the hidden things of darkness and reveal the counsels of the hearts. Then

each one's praise will come from God.
(vv. 4–5)

One final passage against judging is taken from the epistle of James:

> [11] *Do not speak evil of one another, brethren. He who speaks evil of a brother and judges his brother, speaks evil of the law and judges the law. But if you judge the law, you are not a doer of the law but a judge.*
>
> [12] *There is one Lawgiver, who is able to save and to destroy. Who are you to judge another?* (James 4:11–12)

James makes a point that many Christians have overlooked: Speaking evil of another believer is judging that believer. As believers, we are specifically warned not to speak evil of each other. Yet many Christians regularly do just that! It is contrary to Scripture.

2

SCRIPTURES ADVOCATING JUDGING

Now let's look at Scripture passages that say we are to judge. First of all, Jesus spoke to the people of His day concerning His claim to be the Messiah:

> *²⁴ Do not judge according to appearance, but judge with righteous judgment.*
>
> (John 7:24)

In this case, Jesus was telling them to judge. Then in 1 Corinthians 5:1–5 Paul wrote:

> *¹ It is actually reported that there is sexual immorality among you, and such sexual immorality as is not even named among the Gentiles—that a man has his father's wife!*

JUDGING: WHEN? WHY? HOW?

² And you are puffed up, and have not rather mourned, that he who has done this deed might be taken away from among you.

³ For I indeed, as absent in body but present in spirit, have already judged (as though I were present) him who has so done this deed.

⁴ In the name of our Lord Jesus Christ, when you are gathered together, along with my spirit, with the power of our Lord Jesus Christ,

⁵ deliver such a one to Satan for the destruction of the flesh, that his spirit may be saved in the day of the Lord Jesus.

(1 Corinthians 5:1–5)

Notice that Paul said he had *"already judged"* and he required the Corinthian Christians to endorse his judgment. Furthermore, he advocated an extremely severe judgment: to deliver a man over to Satan.

¹¹ But now I have written to you not to keep company with anyone named a brother, who is sexually immoral, or covetous, or an idolater, or a reviler [uses abusive language], or a drunkard, or an extortioner; not even to eat with such a person.

¹² For what have I to do with judging those also who are outside? Do you not judge those who are inside?

¹³ But those who are outside God judges.
(1 Corinthians 5:11–13)

When Paul wrote of *"those who are outside,"* to whom was he referring? Unbelievers. And who did he describe as *"those who are inside"?* Believers. In this instance, therefore, he was saying that we are not responsible to judge unbelievers, but we are required to judge our fellow believers.

¹ Dare any of you, having a matter against another, go to law before the unrighteous, and not before the saints?

² Do you not know that the saints will judge the world? And if the world will be judged by you, are you unworthy to judge the smallest matters?

³ Do you not know that we shall judge angels? How much more, things that pertain to this life?

⁴ If then you have judgments concerning things pertaining to this life, do you appoint those to judge who are least esteemed by the church to judge?
(1 Corinthians 6:1–4)

JUDGING: WHEN? WHY? HOW?

> *⁶ But brother goes to law against brother, and that before unbelievers!*
>
> *⁷ Now therefore, it is already an utter failure for you that you go to law against one another. Why do you not rather accept wrong? Why do you not rather let yourselves be cheated?* (1 Corinthians 6:6–7)

Paul here established two points. First, on the negative side: It is wrong for a Christian to take a fellow Christian to law before a non-Christian court. On the positive side, however, Christians are required to judge internal disputes between fellow Christians.

Finally, look at the words of Jesus in Matthew 18:15–17:

> *¹⁵ Moreover if your brother sins against you, go and tell him his fault between you and him alone. If he hears you, you have gained your brother.*
>
> *¹⁶ But if he will not hear, take with you one or two more, that "by the mouth of two or three witnesses every word may be established."*
>
> *¹⁷ And if he refuses to hear them, tell it to the church.*

Notice again, this is a dispute between believers. If they cannot settle it between themselves, ultimately it has to go before the church. That is not an option; it is a commandment. We are not free to leave disputes unresolved. If we can resolve them as individuals between ourselves, good. Otherwise, we are obligated to take them before the church.

> *17 But if he refuses even to hear the church, let him be to you like a heathen and a tax collector.* (Matthew 18:17)

A man who will not receive the decision of the church loses his right to be treated as a believer. This is a solemn statement!

3
THE RESOLUTION OF THE PARADOX

In the passages we have just looked at, we see that the Scripture places on us an obligation to judge. But the passages we looked at earlier warn us *against* judging. What is the explanation?

I have come to accept a basic principle that resolves this apparent paradox—a principle we must understand in order to discern in any given situation whether we should or should not judge. The principle, simply stated, is this: *Judging is a function of ruling, descending downward from God Himself.*

It is sometimes hard for American Christians to understand this principle because the American Constitution, by design, separates judging from ruling. The executive branch rules, and the judicial branch judges. But this is a separation that has no basis in Scripture.

Let me hasten to add that I am not attacking the Constitution! Since the year 1970, when I became an American citizen, it has been my sincere intention to uphold the Constitution. But when we look at judging from the point of view of the American Constitution, we do not understand judging from God's point of view, because the Bible always unites the two responsibilities of ruling and judging. This link goes back to the very nature of God Himself and is imparted from Him downward into the human race.

In human society, in various areas and on various levels, God has appointed men as judges. In the history of Israel, judging and ruling were never divorced from one another. The book of Judges is the first book describing people who ruled within the area of Israel's inheritance. Judges were Israel's rulers. After that, her rulers became her judges. During the period under the kings, there was no Supreme Court to which anybody could appeal the king's judgment. He was both king and judge, and his judgment was final. Judging and ruling in the Old Testament, then, were never separated. In fact, the sacred word for God, *Elohim,* is actually applied to men who were judges.

THE RESOLUTION OF THE PARADOX

¹ God stands in the congregation of the mighty; He judges among the gods.

⁶ I said, "You are gods, And all of you are children of the Most High."

(Psalm 82:1, 6)

⁶ Then his master shall bring him to the judges. (Exodus 21:6)

⁸ If the thief is not found, then the master of the house shall be brought to the judges to see whether he has put his hand into his neighbor's goods.

⁹ For any kind of trespass, whether it concerns an ox, a donkey, a sheep, or clothing, or for any kind of lost thing which another claims to be his, the cause of both parties shall come before the judges; and whomever the judges condemn shall pay double to his neighbor. (Exodus 22:8–9)

Why were they called gods? Because their function as judges was to take God's place and to judge His people. Their authority came from God, as long as they rightly administered His law.

That the Scripture applies to human judges *Elohim,* the word for the one true God, is a measure of the tremendous sanctity and authority that God attaches to the position of a judge. Several Scriptures make this clear.

JUDGING: WHEN? WHY? HOW?

When God announced to Abraham His intention to judge Sodom, the patriarch actually challenged Him as to whether it was going to be a just judgment. He said,

> *25 Far be it from You to do such a thing as this, to slay the righteous with the wicked, so that the righteous should be as the wicked; far be it from You! Shall not the Judge of all the earth do right?*
>
> (Genesis 18:25)

Who is the Judge of all the earth? God. The Ruler is also the Judge. Notice the important principle established right at the beginning of the Bible—a principle that I believe holds throughout Scripture: *It is contrary to justice to treat the righteous as the wicked.*

Our contemporary Western culture has a negative attitude toward judging. It resents authority and law enforcement. It assumes that the primary function of judging is to punish the wicked. It is not; that is secondary. The primary function of judging is to protect the righteous.

But that concept has been lost sight of in our contemporary culture. The agencies responsible for administering justice bend over backward to protect the criminal and offer little protection to the victim. This is a typical instance of perverted thinking in our modern culture! We must always bear in mind that the primary function of justice is to protect the righteous. It is never in line with God's will to deal with the righteous as with the wicked.

In this connection let me make a parenthetical observation that has a direct bearing on how we treat the matter of divorce. I believe it is contrary to Scripture to treat the innocent party the same as the guilty. That is a denial of the basic principle of Scripture. In the words of Abraham:

> 25 *Far be it from You to do such a thing... that the righteous should be as the wicked; far be it from You! Shall not the Judge of all the earth do right?*　　　(Genesis 18:25)

God responded to Abraham, by implication, "That's right, Abraham: I will never depart from that principle." We see, then, that God the Ruler is also the Judge of all the earth. This principle that never separates judging from ruling will help us later to understand where we should judge and where we should not.

In the psalms, God reproved the judges of Israel:

> 1 *God stands in the congregation of the mighty; He judges among the gods.*
> 　　　　　　　　　　　(Psalm 82:1)

JUDGING: WHEN? WHY? HOW?

What a remarkable statement! Who are *"the gods"?* The judges. Why is God judging them? Because they have been unjust judges, as the passage further states:

> ² *How long will you judge unjustly, and show partiality to the wicked? Selah*
>
> ³ *Defend the poor and fatherless; do justice to the afflicted and needy.* (Psalm 82:2–3)

The primary obligation of a judge, you see, is to protect the righteous:

> ⁴ *Deliver the poor and needy; free them from the hand of the wicked.*
>
> ⁵ *They do not know, nor do they understand.* [In other words, these people will not listen!] *They walk about in darkness; all the foundations of the earth are unstable.* (vv. 4–5)

Another remarkable statement! To me it indicates that when judgment is no longer just, the structure of society is out of line. The whole of society becomes unstable. Stability depends on just judgment.

In the sixth verse, God was speaking:

> ⁶ *I said, "You are gods."*

Why were they called *"gods"*? Because as judges they were representing God to His people.

> [6] *And all of you are children of the Most High.*
>
> [7] *But you shall die like men, and fall like one of the princes.* (Psalm 82:6–7)

Why would this judgment come upon them? Because they had abused their position as judges and had perverted justice.

In the last verse the psalmist said,

> [8] *Arise, O God, judge the earth; for You shall inherit all nations.* (v. 8)

What the psalmist was saying, in effect, is this: "We have not had justice from human judges, so reassert Your right, God, to judge. We need just judgment."

4

THE DELEGATION OF JUDGMENTAL AUTHORITY

As we look on into the New Testament, we find a more detailed picture of judgment.

> *17 And if you call on the Father, who without partiality judges according to each one's work, conduct yourselves throughout the time of your stay here in fear.*
>
> (1 Peter 1:17)

Peter was saying that the One we call Father judges every person according to his work. So the ultimate Judge is God the Father.

In the divine plan, however, God has delegated the office of Judge to Jesus Christ, as Jesus Himself explained:

JUDGING: WHEN? WHY? HOW?

> *²² For the Father judges no one, but has committed all judgment to the Son.*
>
> (John 5:22)

In Matthew 25:31–32 we are given a vivid picture of Jesus establishing His kingdom on earth at the close of this age.

> *³¹ When the Son of Man comes in His glory, and all the holy angels with Him, then He will sit on the throne of His glory.* (v. 31)

Jesus is here depicted as taking His place as Ruler on His throne. What is the first thing He will do as Ruler? He will judge.

> *³² All nations will be gathered before Him, and He will separate them one from another, as a shepherd divides his sheep from the goats.* (v. 32)

We see that Jesus' first public function as the God-appointed Ruler at the close of this age will be to judge those whom He rules. Ruling and judging go together.

But Scripture reveals that there is a downward process of transmitting the Authority to judge. *"For the Father judges no one, but has committed all judgment to the Son"* (John 5:22). The Father is the ultimate authority, the ultimate Ruler, the ultimate Judge. But

He has delegated the function of judging to His Son, Jesus Christ.

Two reasons for this delegation are given. First, *"that all should honor the Son just as they honor the Father"* (John 5:23). In order to make sure the human race pays due honor to the Son, God has made Him the Judge.

In a properly established legal system, in any court of law, one person is honored above all others. Who is that? The judge. This is how it is, too, in the system of authority God has established. Jesus as Judge is honored above all others.

The second reason given in John 5 for Jesus being made the Judge is that the Father *"has given Him authority to execute judgment also, **because He is the Son of Man**"* (v. 27, emphasis added). Jesus is a Judge who can understand our human frailties and infirmities; He experienced them Himself.

> [15] *For we do not have a High Priest who cannot sympathize with our weaknesses, but was in all points tempted as we are, yet without sin.*　　　(Hebrews 4:15)

When we are confronted by some temptation that we consider irresistible, we will never be able to say to Jesus, "But You don't understand!" He has experienced every temptation that is common to man and was never enticed into sin.

But the delegation of authority goes still further. Just as God the Father delegated to the Son authority to judge, so the Son delegated authority to His own Word. Jesus said:

> [48] *He who rejects Me, and does not receive My words, has that which judges him; the word that I have spoken will judge him in the last day.* (John 12:48)

Jesus was saying, "I don't judge anybody; it is My Word that will judge." There is a final delegation of judgmental authority, then, to the Word of God.

5
JUDGING WITHOUT AUTHORITY

Almost all of us may find ourselves strongly tempted at some time to pronounce judgment on people who are obviously doing things they have no right to do. But Scripture provides examples that warn us against stepping beyond the limits of our authority to judge. First, we will look at the account of Lot in the city of Sodom.

You remember the story. Lot had gone to Sodom as a visitor and settled in the city but had never been given any official position. The men of Sodom, who were very wicked, wanted to have sex with the angels who had come to Lot's house, and Lot was reproving them. But the men he was trying to restrain responded in this way:

⁹ And they said, "Stand back!" Then they said, "This one came in to stay here, and he keeps acting as a judge; now we will deal worse with you than with them."

(Genesis 19:9)

In effect, they were saying to Lot, "You have no authority to judge. Nobody made you a judge in this city; you're just a visitor. Don't try to tell us what to do!"

From the legal point of view, these men were right, although of course their conduct was abominable. Through his own foolishness Lot had put himself into a position where he was a witness to evil deeds while he had no authority to restrain. Fortunately for him, the angelic visitors intervened on his behalf.

Now take the case of Moses. At the age of forty, self-appointed, he set out to deliver Israel from its slavery in Egypt. The first day he killed an Egyptian who was mistreating one of his fellow Israelites. The next day he found two Israelites fighting and tried to administer judgment to them. But they did not listen to him. So Moses said to the man who was doing wrong to his fellow Israelite:

¹³ "Why are you striking your companion?"

¹⁴ Then the man said, "Who made you a prince [ruler] and a judge over us? Do you intend to kill me as you killed the Egyptian?"   (Exodus 2:13–14)

He had a point: Moses had no authority. Nobody had made him a ruler. He had no right, therefore, to judge. Moses ended up running away for forty years of exile in the desert.

There in exile, at the age of eighty, Moses experienced a life-transforming encounter with the Lord. When he returned to Egypt as God's appointed ruler, he had authority not merely to judge the people of Israel, but also to perform a series of miracles unequalled by any other human being.

This idea carries over into the New Testament. In Luke 12:13–14, Jesus was confronted by a man who claimed he was being cheated out of his inheritance by his brother. In reply, Jesus actually quoted the words of the Israelite to Moses and applied them to Himself: *"Man, who made Me a judge or an arbitrator over you?"* (v. 14).

In effect, Jesus was saying, "There's a court here to take care of cases like that. There are elders; there is a Sanhedrin. I don't have any authority in this area; I can't judge you." Do you see the wisdom of the Lord? Although Jesus was the Son of God and God's representative, He did not have authority in this area, so He did not judge. How many of us would be as wise?

6
JUDGING AND RULING

We have seen that there is a logical and inseparable link between ruling and judging. Primarily this is revealed in the eternal nature of God Himself. He is both the Supreme Ruler and the Supreme Judge.

The same principle applies, however, to all those on the human level who have the responsibility to rule. In every area where they are given responsibility to rule, they must also be given responsibility to judge.

If you give your oldest daughter the responsibility to baby-sit your younger children, you must also give her the authority to judge—that is, to apply the rules that determine what behavior is acceptable and what is not permitted. She must determine, for instance, which TV programs they are permitted to watch and which they are not. Otherwise, her job becomes impossible.

JUDGING: WHEN? WHY? HOW?

These are two things that must never be separated: responsibility and authority. When a person is given responsibility to rule, he or she must also be given authority to judge. We cannot divorce the one from the other. Responsibility without authority is ineffective. Authority without responsibility is despotism.

We can then establish these simple, basic principles:

- *Where we have the responsibility to rule, we also have the authority to judge.*

- *Conversely, where we do not have the responsibility to rule, we do not have the authority to judge.*

However, we must take our analysis a step further. Let us suppose that we have answered to our satisfaction the question of *who* is authorized to judge. There is still one further vital question. *What* is that person authorized to judge? Does that person have unlimited authority to judge every issue that arises? Or is his authority limited to certain defined areas?

To return for a moment to the example of the eldest daughter baby-sitting her younger siblings, she has authority to determine what TV programs they may watch. But does she also have authority to determine what books they may read? Or are they perhaps permitted to read any book they may choose out of a library carefully assembled by their parents?

Let me illustrate the concept of limited authority from personal experience. Some years ago a Jewish attorney walked past the tennis court in Florida where I used to play and invited me to play tennis with him. After that we started playing together regularly. Later he was elected to the County Court, so I found myself playing tennis with a judge! He explained to me the responsibilities he felt in his new office.

"The maximum penalty I am entitled to give is one year in prison," he said. "That's the limit of my authority. Believe it or not, I find it so exhausting trying to do my job right that I go to bed at eight o'clock every night!"

His new situation was a good example of limited authority to judge. What was the area of his authority? Only one county, Broward County. He had no authority in Dade County or Palm Beach County. What kind of people was he authorized to judge? Only those who committed offenses for which the maximum penalty was less than one year in prison. Other kinds of criminals fell outside of his judgment.

What was he entitled to judge? Anything contrary to Florida law or the statutes or ordinances of Broward County. If a man was driving thiry-five miles an hour in a thirty-mile-an-hour zone, for instance, my tennis friend was entitled to judge him for that act. But if the same man was driving thirty miles an hour in his convertible with the hood down, my friend could not judge him for that act since it was not an offense. His authority to judge was confined to a certain area and to certain kinds of people doing certain kinds of things.

This type of limitation is typical of all judgment, and the principle applies, practically speaking, to all of us. There is an area, there are people and there are acts, that we must judge. Outside of that area, and with other people, and with different acts, we have no authority to judge.

Our discussion of judgment is not complete, then, until we answer all three questions: *In what areas are we authorized to judge? Whom are we authorized to judge? And what are the offenses that we are authorized to judge?* We may have authority to judge certain people but not about certain things. And if we judge those people for things we are not authorized to judge, we are exceeding our authority.

We will discuss the answer to each of these three questions. But first there are several things we are *never* responsible to judge.

7

WHAT WE ARE NOT RESPONSIBLE TO JUDGE

We are not responsible for the final evaluation of anyone's character, including our own.

It was a great relief to me when I discovered I was not responsible for making judgments of this kind, because, frankly, like most religious people, I had been doing a lot of it. It was a heavy responsibility, and it was getting more and more difficult to be sure I was right. Then one day I realized I did not have to do it at all!

Let's go back to 1 Corinthians 4 for an example of this principle. The first two verses are introductory:

JUDGING: WHEN? WHY? HOW?

¹ Let a man so consider us, as servants of Christ and stewards of the mysteries of God.

² Moreover it is required in stewards that one be found faithful.

(1 Corinthians 4:1–2)

The word *steward* leads to the thought of judging, because a steward is answerable to the one he serves for the way he conducts his stewardship. He will be judged according to whether or not he has been faithful. Paul was saying, "My fellow ministers and I will be judged for whether we have been faithful stewards of the mysteries of God." Then he continued,

³ But with me it is a very small thing that I should be judged by you or by a human court. In fact, I do not even judge myself.

(v. 3)

In the area that Paul was talking about, he said, "You don't judge me, I don't judge you, I don't even judge myself. This is an area of judgment not left in our hands at all."

We are not required to judge or make a final evaluation of the absolute value of anybody, including ourselves.

WHAT WE ARE NOT RESPONSIBLE TO JUDGE

> *⁴ For I know of nothing against myself; yet I am not justified by this; but He who judges me is the Lord.* (1 Corinthians 4:4)

This is better translated: "I am not conscious of anything against myself; I don't know of anything that I've done wrong. But that doesn't justify me, because I am not the Judge; God is the Judge. He knows things about me that I don't know about myself."

Here is an area in which the Lord alone is the Judge. Let me restate the principle: *We are never responsible for the final evaluation of anyone's character or conduct—including our own.* The final evaluation, the great summing up of our whole life, will be made by none other than the Lord Himself.

> *⁵ Therefore judge nothing before the time, until the Lord comes, who will both bring to light the hidden things of darkness and reveal the counsels of the hearts.* (1 Corinthians 4:5)

We are specifically warned not to judge things *"before the time."* What time is that? The time when the Lord will do the judging. This judgment will take place only when the Lord comes. Why is the Lord the only One who can judge in this area of human conduct and character? Because nobody else knows all the secrets of human hearts and motives.

JUDGING: WHEN? WHY? HOW?

This is why we are never responsible for the final evaluation of anyone's character—including our own—because God *"will both bring to light the hidden things of darkness and reveal the counsels of the hearts"* (1 Corinthians 4:5).

When it comes to judging a person's inner personality, the only One who knows all the truth is God. And without knowing all the truth, we are not able to judge accurately or fairly. We are not qualified to judge others. We are not qualified to judge even ourselves. Only the Lord knows our motives. He knows how honest we have been. He knows when we have been hypocritical or insincere. He knows everything. He alone is qualified to judge.

Finally, Paul said:

[5] *Then each one's praise will come from God.* (v. 5)

God's ultimate purpose is not to condemn us but to praise us and reward us for everything good we have done. Let's wait patiently for that wonderful moment!

8

THE JUDGMENT SEAT
OF CHRIST

Let's look a little further at the kind of judgment that nobody shares with God—the judgment that is exclusively His.

Paul spoke about *"the day when God will judge the secrets of men by Jesus Christ, according to my gospel"* (Romans 2:16).

To whom did Paul refer? To all believers. This is not a judgment of unbelievers, or a judgment for condemnation, because *"there is therefore now no condemnation to those who are in Christ Jesus"* (Romans 8:1). Rather, this is a judgment of believers to evaluate our service. It is to this judgment that Peter referred in 1 Peter 4:17:

JUDGING: WHEN? WHY? HOW?

17 For the time has come for judgment to begin at the house of God; and if it begins with us first, what will be the end of those who do not obey the gospel of God?

The phrase *"the house of God"* denotes the true Christians who are God's temple. Speaking as a Christian, Peter also referred to them as *"us."* Before the unbelievers are judged, the believers will be brought before the judgment seat of Christ.

Paul also referred to this judgment of believers also in 2 Corinthians 5:10:

10 For we must all appear before the judgment seat of Christ, that each one may receive the things done in the body, according to what he has done, whether good or bad.

"We...all" refers to believers in Christ. More literally, this verse could be translated, "We must all be *made manifest."* Everything will be brought out into the awesome light of God's countenance. There will be no secrets, no alibis, and no excuses.

No wonder Paul continued, *"Knowing, therefore, the terror of the Lord, we persuade men; but we are well known* [literally, "we have been made manifest"] *to God"* (2 Corinthians 5:11). By repeating the Greek word meaning "to make manifest," Paul empha-sized that everything will be brought out into the Light. There will be nothing that is not laid bare.

Furthermore, all our actions fall into one or the other of two categories: either *"good or bad"* (2 Corinthians 5:10). There is nothing neutral. Anything that is not good is bad.

In 1 John 5:17 we are confronted with the same dichotomy: *"All unrighteousness is sin."* Whatever is not positively righteous is actually sinful. There is no neutral ground between righteousness and sin.

In Romans 14:12, Paul applied this prin-ciple in a direct and personal way to each individual Christian:

12 So then each of us shall give account of himself to God.

Once we grasp the certainty and solem-nity of appearing before the judgment seat of Christ, we will be so occupied with making and keeping ourselves ready that we will have little time left for passing final judgment on other people.

We will be particularly careful of the effect that our lives have on other people. Paul emphasized this idea in Romans 14:13:

JUDGING: WHEN? WHY? HOW?

¹³ Therefore let us not judge one another anymore, but rather resolve this, not to put a stumbling block or a cause to fall in our brother's way.

This is important. Conduct that causes a fellow believer to stumble or turn aside is something for which we will be judged. Do you remember what Jesus said about anyone who offends one of the little ones who believe in Him?

⁶ It would be better for him if a millstone were hung around his neck, and he were drowned in the depth of the sea.
(Matthew 18:6)

The judgment confronting that person is terrible to contemplate!

The New Testament warns us that, as Christians, we will all stand before the judgment seat of Christ. Some contemporary preachers seldom talk about judgment. For my part, whenever I study this theme of judgment in order to preach about it, it has a powerful personal impact on the way I live.

One thing modern man hates is to be told that he is accountable. Our contemporary culture and philosophy are often undercover ways to reject accountability! One main reason that people want to believe the theory of evolution is that it does not confront us with a personal Creator to whom we must all give account for the lives we have been leading.

Yet in spite of all our theories and all our arguments, we come face-to-face with one inescapable fact: There is a Creator who is also a Judge, to whom we will all give an account.

It is not merely our actions, however, that will be judged, but also our motives. There is only one legitimate motive for anything we ever do: *"Therefore, whether you eat or drink, or whatever you do, **do all to the glory of God"*** (1 Corinthians 10:31, emphasis added). If there is anything that we cannot do to the glory of God, probably we should not be doing it at all.

In particular, Paul specified the simple, familiar acts of eating and drinking. Frankly, I have to say I think some people would change their eating habits if their aim were to eat to the glory of God. Yet the Bible says that is what God requires. Do we realize that we are going to give account for the way we eat?

In Hebrews 6:1–2 the writer lists the six foundational doctrines of the Christian church. The sixth and final doctrine is *eternal judgment.* This is the climax of every human life, the "exit" through which we will all pass out of time into eternity. Very little is taught today in many places about the fact that we are going to answer to God personally for the lives we have led. Yet for many years I myself have lived my life with this consciousness that I will have to answer to God for what I say and do, and it has had a powerful effect on the way I live. I believe eternal judgment is one of the foundational doctrines because it is so important in determining the way we live.

But this judgment belongs only to God.

9

WHAT ARE WE RESPONSIBLE TO JUDGE?

Up to this point we have reviewed certain areas in which God alone has the authority to judge. Now we will look at certain other areas in which God holds us responsible to judge.

The first area is this: We are responsible to judge our personal conduct and relationships.

We have already seen that we are not to make a final evaluation of either ourselves or others. The judgment we are required to make, therefore, is not an absolute evaluation of any person's worth, but it is essentially a judgment of conduct. We are to judge conduct not by our feelings, or by the opinions of society, or even by our own estimate of ourselves. We *are* responsible to judge our conduct and relationships by the clear teaching and standards revealed in the Word of God.

We saw earlier that just as God the Father delegated to the Son the authority to judge, so the Son in turn delegated authority to His own Word. By what standard, therefore, are we to judge ourselves? By the same standard God uses: His own Word.

In 1 Corinthians 11:28–32 Paul gave instructions about celebrating the Lord's Supper:

> *28 But let a man examine himself, and so let him eat of the bread and drink of the cup.* (v. 28)

We are warned that before we partake of the Lord's Supper we should examine ourselves. By what standard? The Word of God. This has become a principle with me: I never take Communion without first examining myself. To do otherwise would be dangerous.

> *29 For he who eats and drinks in an unworthy manner eats and drinks judgment to himself, not discerning the Lord's body.*

> *30 For this reason many are weak and sick among you, and many sleep* [that is, have died untimely]. (vv. 29–30)

WHAT ARE WE RESPONSIBLE TO JUDGE?

This is a solemn fact! If we do not examine ourselves before partaking of Communion, we are liable to bring on ourselves sickness and even untimely death.

> [31] *For if we would judge ourselves, we would not be judged.*
>
> (1 Corinthians 11:31)

If we judge ourselves, we will not be judged by God. But if we do not judge ourselves, Paul said, and we take the Lord's Supper unworthily, then God will judge us. The option is ours: If we judge ourselves, we preempt God's judgment. He will not judge us in those areas in which we have correctly judged ourselves.

There are three alternatives, then, in descending order of desirability:

1. Judge yourself and do not come under God's judgment.

2. Fail to judge yourself and come under God's judgment, but let this prompt you to repentance.

3. Come under God's judgment, fail to repent, and be judged with the unbelievers.

Each of us will experience judgment in one of the above forms.

JUDGING: WHEN? WHY? HOW?

Paul mentioned two ways God judged the Christians in Corinth because they had failed to judge themselves. Some were sick and others had died before their time. We need to bear in mind that the sickness and premature deaths of those believers were a judgment of God because they had not judged themselves. Obviously, to have prayed for healing or health in such cases would have been ineffective.

We are responsible, then, to judge our own conduct and relationships. And if we judge ourselves by the Word of God, bringing our lives into line with His Word, then God has nothing to judge us for.

Here are some questions that I personally ask myself before taking Communion: Am I at peace with my brother or sister? Do I harbor bitterness or resentment in my heart? Have I spoken evil of my fellow believer? Have I said things about him or her that were either untrue or uncharitable? These are some of the ways in which I believe we are all obligated to judge ourselves.

If we would take seriously our responsibility to judge ourselves, we would have less time to judge others whom we are not supposed to judge!

10
JUDGING OTHERS

Let us suppose that we have accepted our responsibility to judge ourselves. Who else are we responsible to judge? We come back to our basic principle: ruling and judging go together. We are responsible to judge those whom we are responsible to rule.

For instance, a husband and father is responsible to judge his family. In this, he should rely upon the counsel and support of his wife as his God-given "helper." Nevertheless, the primary responsibility rests upon the man.

First Timothy 3:4–5 speaks about the qualifications of an elder—one who is to rule the church. It lists, among other qualifications: *"One who rules his own house well, having his children in submission with all reverence (for if a man does not know how to rule his own house, how will he take care of the church of God?)"*

A man's family is the proving ground for his public ministry. When he can rule effectively at home, he becomes a candidate for promotion to public leadership. But if he cannot rule effectively at home, he is not qualified for public leadership. There is a direct relationship between a man's position in his family and the position of an elder or ruler in the church. Each is ruling in his particular area, so each is obligated to judge.

What conduct is a father or husband responsible to judge? Again, let me say that none of us is responsible for the final evaluation of the worth of any other person. A husband is not responsible for the final evaluation of his wife's eternal worth, nor a father for the final evaluation of the eternal worth of his children.

What, then, is a husband or father required to judge? He must judge conduct that affects the welfare of those for whom he is responsible.

If I see my children continually indulging in soft drinks, ice cream, and candy, I must warn them that they are in danger of ruining their teeth and their health. To ensure that they grow up healthy, I may have to make rules that limit their indulgence in those things.

Or if I see my child reading a certain kind of book—maybe ghost stories—and he or she is already nervous and does not sleep well at night, that kind of reading is absolutely the last thing that is suitable for that particular child! I have an obligation to say, "I don't want to see any more of those books in your bedroom, and I want to know what you're reading."

I am also obligated to judge conduct that affects the honor and order of our home. I will be held accountable by God and probably also by my neighbors. If my children are rude and undisciplined, it reflects on me as the father. It indicates that I am not fulfilling my function. The Danish have a saying, "The apple doesn't fall far from the tree." That is a neat way of observing that what parents are like is usually what their children will turn out to be also.

One of the words that has almost dropped out of use today is *honor*. Yet a father should be concerned about the honor of his family and his home. The children of a friend of mine, a well-known preacher, were misbehaving. He said to them, "I want you to know that the name you bear is a very honorable name, and you are responsible for what people think about it." That turned his children around!

11
THOSE IN THE CHURCH

The next area of judgment is the main one dealt with in the New Testament: the church, the corporate body of believers. Remember that leaders are expected to judge those whom they lead. Hebrews 13:7 and 13:17 were addressed to church members but indicate what is expected of their leaders:

> *7 Remember those who rule over you* [or who lead you], *who have spoken the word of God to you, whose faith follow, considering the outcome of their conduct* [that is, the results you see in their lives].

> *17 Obey those who rule over you, and be submissive, for they watch out for your souls.*

It is clear that the church leadership is expected to exercise authority and maintain discipline. In fact, where there is no leadership that performs these functions, it is not correct, in a scriptural sense, to talk about a church. In Acts 14:21–23, groups of disciples became churches only when elders were appointed. Before the elders were appointed, they were just groups of disciples. It took leadership to make them into a church. Where there is no effective leadership, you may have a meeting, but the New Testament would not acknowledge that as a church.

The Greek word for church is *ecclesia*. The normal meaning of this, in contemporary secular literature, was a "governmental assembly." In Acts 19, for instance, the city of Ephesus was governed by its *ecclesia*, its assembly. The word *ecclesia* is translated three times in Acts 19 as *"assembly"* (vv. 32, 39, 41). In other words, the very essence of the Church—the *ecclesia*—is governmental. Without government, nothing justifies the use of the word *church*.

As we look back over history as far as the Reformation, we see a division in Christianity in our Western world. One stream remained Catholic, the other became Protestant. Ever since, Catholics and Protestants have been busy pointing out one another's errors. A Catholic friend of mine once asked, "Wouldn't it be better if we changed, each focusing on the good points of the other and straightening out our own errors?"

Whether we are Catholic or Protestant by background, we often have certain preconceptions that we have never fully examined. One common error of Protestantism, I observe, is that everybody thinks he has a right to judge in every situation.

Corrie ten Boom from Holland, one of the countries torn most bitterly by the conflict between Catholics and Protestants, said to me once, "Every Dutchman is his own theologian." That may be particularly characteristic of the Dutch people, but it describes a feature that is common to Protestantism as a whole. Without appropriate safeguards, however, this can lead to instability and fragmentation.

Ultimately, although the church is under leadership, the final responsibility for judgment does not rest merely with the leaders. In most areas where the New Testament holds us as Christians accountable to judge, it addresses us in the plural, not in the singular. In other words, we are responsible to judge collectively, not individually.

Let's look at a few of the Scriptures that tell us what we are responsible to judge. In every case, as far as I can determine, it is the collective body of believers that is responsible to do the judging.

12
MORAL STANDARDS

In 1 Corinthians 5 Paul spoke about the moral standards that a congregation is required to maintain:

¹ It is actually reported that there is sexual immorality among you, and such sexual immorality as is not even named among the Gentiles; that a man has his father's wife!

² And you are puffed up, and have not rather mourned, that he who has done this deed might be taken away from among you.

³ For I indeed, as absent in body but present in spirit, have already judged (as though I were present) him who has so done this deed.   (vv. 1–3)

The Corinthians were puffed up with their spiritual gifts but did not deal with sin.

Unfortunately, this is often true of churches that place an excessive emphasis on spiritual gifts that is not balanced by the discipline of Scripture. Paul told the Corinthians plainly that a man guilty of such conduct had no place in the church. But although Paul gave his judgment as an apostle, it required the endorsement of the church as a whole. That was why he was writing, urging them:

> *4 In the name of our Lord Jesus Christ, when you are gathered together, along with my spirit, with the power* [authority] *of our Lord Jesus Christ,*

> *5 deliver such a one to Satan for the destruction of the flesh, that his spirit may be saved in the day of the Lord Jesus.*
> (1 Corinthians 5:4–5)

That was a fearful judgment! But notice the words *"when you are gathered together,"* referring to the collective action of the whole body. Paul was saying he could not be there in person but was coming through his letter and would be praying. "When you act," he said, "my spirit will be acting with you."

What does it mean to deliver a person to Satan? I confess there are areas in which I do not have full understanding. But Satan is *"the god of this age"* (2 Corinthians 4:4). When a person is excluded from the body of believers, he or she is turned out into the world. What a terrible destiny! It does not necessarily mean that we say, "Satan, we hand this person over to you." Nevertheless, to be excluded from the fellowship of God's people is, in a certain sense, to be handed over to Satan.

The man being dealt with in this case was guilty of both adultery and incest. Further in the same chapter, Paul expanded the list of sins that have to be dealt with:

> *9 I wrote to you in my epistle not to keep company with sexually immoral people.*
>
> *10 Yet I certainly did not mean with the sexually immoral people of this world, or with the covetous, or extortioners, or idolaters, since you would need to go out of the world.*
>
> *11 But now I have written to you not to keep company with anyone named a brother, who is sexually immoral, or covetous, or an idolater, or a reviler, or a drunkard, or an extortioner—not even to eat with such a person.* (1 Corinthians 5:9–11)

Writing in the first century of our era, Paul was realistic about the condition of the world around him. For a Christian to separate himself completely from the kinds of people whom Paul described—the sexually immoral, the covetous, the idolater, the reviler (abusive person), the drunkard, and the extortioner (swindler)—such a Christian would have to break off contact with the world.

A realistic view of the world around us as the twenty-first century opens would lead us to the same conclusion. We are surrounded by people who are sinners in thought and word and deed. The world has not changed, and it will never change. Only the grace of God in Christ can effect the kind of radical change that is needed.

As Christians, however, we are not required to take responsibility for the behavior of the people of the world around us. Therefore, we are not required to judge their conduct.

When the person I relate to professes to be a Christian, however, the situation is different. If I am known to be a Christian and I maintain close fellowship with a person such as Paul described, the unbeliever who knows us both will conclude that I accept that person as a fellow Christian. I will be giving him a false picture of what it means to be a Christian. I will be compromising my own testimony.

For this reason Paul said,

8 Live as children of light

10 and find out what pleases the Lord.

11 Have nothing to do with the fruitless deeds of darkness, but rather expose them.
(Ephesians 5:8, 10–11 NIV)

To be open and honest, I have to say to such a person, "As long as you continue to live the way you are, I won't fellowship with you. Because, if I did, the world would think that I accept you as my fellow Christian, and I would be deceiving the world as to what a Christian really is. Until you change your lifestyle, I can't continue to fellowship with you."

Paul summed this situation up by saying:

12 For what have I to do with judging those who are outside? Do you not judge those who are inside?

13 But those who are outside God judges.
(1 Corinthians 5:12–13)

What did Paul mean by *"those who are inside"?* Our fellow believers. On the other hand, you do not have to judge *"those who are outside,"* that is, the unbelievers.

Throughout this passage the pronoun *"you"* is plural. It is the corporate responsibility of the collective church to judge such matters.

In conclusion, Paul demanded strong disciplinary action by the church as a whole.

> *13 Therefore put away from yourselves the evil person.*   (1 Corinthians 5:13)

The situation that Paul was dealing with was an unusual case of immorality that does not happen in every church every day. On the other hand, I have frequently encountered, in the course of visiting various churches, cases of incest between father and daughter and cases of practicing homosexuality among members. This behavior is not something remote from another age. In fact, we are liable to be faced with more and more of it as the morality of our own society deteriorates.

Somebody once said, "A ship in the sea is all right; but the sea in the ship is all wrong." The church in the world is all right. The world in the church is all wrong. One main purpose of discipline is to keep the world out of the church. But it is a continual battle!

13

DISPUTES BETWEEN BELIEVERS

What else, besides ethical and moral conduct, are we responsible to judge? We are also responsible to judge disputes between believers. The Scriptures are clear about this. To start with, let's turn to the words of Jesus in Matthew 18:15: *"If your brother sins against you."*

Would borrowing two thousand dollars, promising to pay it back within thirty days, and keeping it six months be a sin? I would say it would. Do Christians ever do such things to one another? They certainly do!

So if this happens to you, what are you to do about it? Go to the attorney? No!

JUDGING: WHEN? WHY? HOW?

15 Go and tell him his fault between you and him alone. If he hears you, you have gained your brother.   (Matthew 18:15)

The first step is to go to the person privately. Do not go to anybody else!

In my experience, in disputes between fellow Christians, at least fifty percent of us start by doing the wrong thing: we go to somebody other than the offending brother. When we do that, the problem gets out of hand.

My first wife, Lydia, was an outspoken person. When she was a missionary in Israel many years ago, before we were married, a certain pastor was very critical of her because she was "Pentecostal." He criticized her to other Christians. Eventually the Lord convicted him, and he came to her to ask her to forgive him. Her answer was typical. "I have to forgive you for my sake," she said. "But go up into a tower with a bag of feathers, and let them out into the wind, and see how many feathers you can get back."

What has been said, in other words, cannot be unsaid. When we misuse our tongues and talk to the wrong people, we are opening a bag of feathers in the wind. How many of them can we get back?

Taking that first step and going to your brother is often surprisingly effective. Years ago, when I was a young Christian, a brother made some unfair remarks about a person very close to me, and I made an appointment to see the brother privately. When we met, his knees were literally knocking with fright! I did not need to scold him or argue with him. In such a case, the scriptural approach can release the authority of God into a situation.

> [16] But if he will not hear, take with you one or two more, that "by the mouth of two or three witnesses every word may be established." (Matthew 18:16)

Here is another principle: *In matters of judgment, everything has to be established by at least two witnesses.* I will say more about this later.

If your brother will not hear the witnesses you bring, what is the next step?

> [17] And if he refuses to hear them, tell it to the church. But if he refuses even to hear the church, let him be to you like a heathen and a tax collector. (v. 17)

Jesus was saying that the one who will not accept the decision of the church forfeits his right to be treated as a Christian.

JUDGING: WHEN? WHY? HOW?

Two things about this frighten me. First, I would be scared to deliberately set aside any decision of a church that had been reached in a scriptural way. The other thing that frightens me is to think of the authority vested in the church, yet how few churches are in any way competent to exercise that authority!

Let's go on to 1 Corinthians 6 and see this principle applied to a church situation:

> *¹ Dare any of you, having a matter against another, go to law before the unrighteous, and not before the saints* [believers]*?*
>
> (v. 1)

"*Dare any of you?*" Notice how strongly Paul felt!

> *² Do you not know that the saints will judge the world? And if the world will be judged by you, are you unworthy to judge the smallest matters?*
>
> *³ Do you not know that we shall judge angels? How much more, things that pertain to this life?*
>
> *⁴ If then you have judgments concerning things pertaining to this life, do you appoint those who are least esteemed by the church to judge?*
>
> *⁵ I say this to your shame. Is it so, that there is not a wise man among you, not even*

*one, who will be able to judge between his
brethren?* (1 Corinthians 6:2–5)

This passage is not saying that a Christian must not go to law. It is saying that a Christian must not go to law with a fellow believer.

We may be tested on this. Some years ago, I bought a house from a believer, and we agreed to use the same lawyer. I will never do that again! The man we chose was a tongues-speaking lawyer. But he was also a crook. In good faith, I paid the money I owed, but the lawyer appropriated the money to pay another debt—his own.

When I discovered what the lawyer had done, I went to him about it. It took me a few weeks to catch up with him! But he was so bankrupt that I had no possibility of ever recovering the money. So I wrote to the man from whom I had bought the house and told him our lawyer had swindled us. Because the money I had paid the lawyer had been diverted to another use, I suggested that we share the loss between us. The fellow believer wrote back and said, "No, you paid the money. It's your loss."

So I consulted a second, more reliable lawyer. He told me that according to his understanding, it was not my loss but the former owner's, because I had bought the house free of encumbrances and was entitled to receive it that way.

Then I had to do some praying! Finally, because the Bible says that we are not to go to court with a fellow believer, I accepted the loss and paid the money a second time. Eventually, the money I lost, God gave me back many times over. But it was a test!

I am not saying that if I had a contract with an unbeliever and he broke it, I would not, after praying it over, go to court. I am saying simply that we are not free to go to law with a fellow believer. It is a reproach if believers take each other before a worldly court. Such disputes should be settled in the church. But how many churches today would be competent to handle such an issue?

A Methodist woman wrote me once complaining that a member of her church had rented some property from her and her husband but was not paying the rent. What was my advice? I quoted 1 Corinthians 6:1–6 and suggested she go to the leaders of her church and state the case before them. I never heard another word from her. I do not think she was pleased with my advice, and I could well believe that the leaders of her church would not have known how to handle that problem. Nevertheless, that is the scriptural procedure.

After I left a church in Canada that I had pastored, the congregation joined with another congregation, then split up. One congregation ended up with all the money, and the other wanted half of it. So they went to law in a civil court. The judge was quoted in the paper as saying, "It is a reproach to you people that I have to judge this case."

14
DOCTRINES AND MINISTRIES

What else are we required to judge? Paul gave another example in Romans 16:17:

> *17 Now I urge you, brethren, note those who cause divisions and offenses, contrary to the doctrine which you learned, and avoid them.*

If people begin to propagate incorrect doctrine, and it becomes a source of division in the church, we are exhorted to notice those people and refuse fellowship to them. The basis for judging and refusing fellowship in this case is doctrinal error that breeds division in the church.

In this case, Paul apparently had in mind some kind of false doctrine that originates within a congregation. On the other hand, false doctrine may also be imported from outside through visiting preachers or teachers.

In Revelation 2:2 Jesus said to the church of Ephesus:

> ² *I know your works, your labor, your patience, and that you cannot bear those who are evil. And you have tested those who say they are apostles and are not, and have found them liars.*

Jesus commended that church because when men came claiming to be apostles, the church collectively tested them and rejected their claim. Though the Ephesian church is addressed in the singular, we understand that it was the whole church collectively that was responsible. It was a very serious decision that they reached, because in Revelation 22:15 the list of those forever excluded from the New Jerusalem and from the Tree of Life concludes with, *"Whoever loves and practices a lie."*

This subject is more fully dealt with in "Appendix 1: How to Recognize Apostles."

15
A WARNING TO DUMB DOGS

In this connection, it is important to observe a distinction between two kinds of problems that may occur. On the one hand, there are personal disputes between individual believers; on the other hand, there are forms of misconduct or errors of doctrine that affect the whole body of Christ.

In dealing with personal disputes, our aim should be to bring about some kind of reconciliation between the parties. Failing that, we should seek at least to seal up the problem between the persons involved, so that it does not develop into a wider dispute affecting more people.

On the other hand, if we are dealing with some kind of serious misconduct or doctrinal error that could poison the whole body of Christ, we must be more concerned for the welfare of the body than for the resolution of personal differences. As shepherds of God's flock, our first concern must be to warn and protect the sheep.

Here are two examples of how the apostles dealt with this kind of situation. Concerning a believer named Hymenaeus, Paul said in 1 Timothy 1:18–20,

> *18 This charge I commit to you, son Timothy, according to the prophecies previously made concerning you, that by them you may wage the good warfare,*

> *19 having faith and a good conscience, which some having rejected, concerning the faith have suffered shipwreck,*

> *20 of whom are Hymenaeus and Alexander, whom I delivered to Satan that they may learn not to blaspheme.*

In 2 Timothy 2:17–18 Paul referred again to Hymenaeus:

> *17 And their message will spread like cancer. Hymenaeus and Philetus are of this sort,*

> *18 who have strayed concerning the truth, saying that the resurrection is already*

*past; and they overthrow the faith of
some.*

Paul saw the error that Hymenaeus was
propagating as a *"cancer"* in the body of Christ,
and he was ruthless in his determination to
cut it out. The Greek word translated *"cancer"*
is the word from which we form the English
word *gangrene*. Paul's concern for the welfare
of Christ's body took precedence over any personal relationship he might have had with
Hymenaeus. He was therefore outspoken in
his public condemnation of Hymenaeus. The
issue to be settled was not a personal relationship between Paul and Hymenaeus, but a doctrinal error affecting the whole body of Christ.

Another example of this principle is found
in 3 John 9–10 where the apostle John
warned the believers against Diotrephes:

> [9] *I wrote to the church, but Diotrephes,
> who loves to have the preeminence among
> them, does not receive us.*

> [10] *Therefore, if I come, I will call to mind
> his deeds which he does, prating against
> us with malicious words. And not content
> with that, he himself does not receive the
> brethren, and forbids those who wish to,
> putting them out of the church.*

Clearly, John felt obligated to warn his fellow
believers because the behavior of Diotrephes

was a cause of disorder and disunity in the body of Christ. John's concern for the body of Christ as a whole was more important than any personal feelings he might have had for Diotrephes as a brother.

It still may happen today that we find ourselves confronted with a situation in which our concern for the body of Christ must take precedence over any personal relationship that we may have with an individual believer.

In Isaiah's time, the Lord charged the leaders of Israel that they were failing in their responsibility to His people:

> *10 They are all dumb dogs, they cannot bark.* (Isaiah 56:10)

At the approach of a predator, it was the duty of the sheepdogs to bark and thus to warn both the shepherds and the sheep. But if the dogs kept silent, they endangered those who looked to them for protection.

The same truth applies to God's people today. Wherever the flock is threatened by doctrinal error or deceptive ministries, it is the solemn responsibility of the leaders to give clear authoritative warning. Leaders who fail in this responsibility are in the same category as the *"dumb dogs"* whom God reproved in Isaiah's time.

There is further information on this subject in "Appendix 2: True and False Prophets."

16

HOW TO IDENTIFY FALSE MINISTRIES

In Matthew 7:15 Jesus warned us concerning false prophets,

> *15 Beware of false prophets, who come to you in sheep's clothing, but inwardly they are ravenous wolves.*

The wolf is the natural enemy of the sheep, while the sheep represent the true believers. The wolf coming in sheep's clothing indicates a deceiver—somebody claiming to be a real Christian, but who is not. Jesus went on to say,

> *16 You will know them by their fruits. Do men gather grapes from thornbushes or figs from thistles?* (v. 16)

JUDGING: WHEN? WHY? HOW?

How many times do we have to prick our fingers on a thorn, hoping to get a grape, before we conclude that someone is a false prophet?

In conclusion, Jesus provided a decisive test: the test of *fruit*.

> *17 Even so, every good tree bears good fruit, but a bad tree bears bad fruit.*

> *18 A good tree cannot bear bad fruit, nor can a bad tree bear good fruit.*

> *19 Every tree that does not bear good fruit is cut down and thrown into the fire.*

> *20 Therefore by their fruits you will know them.* (Matthew 7:17–20)

The difference between fruit and gifts may be illustrated by comparing a Christmas tree with an apple tree. The *gifts* on a Christmas tree are placed there by a single act, and are likewise taken from it by a single act. No process of maturing or ripening is required.

On the other hand, the *fruit* of an apple tree is produced by a process that extends over a period of time. This process includes planting, watering, tending, pruning, and ultimately collecting the fruit. There is no such thing as instant fruit.

In the spiritual realm, the fruit we should look for is Christian character. This character is developed by a process that includes testing and discipline. The end product is a *disciple*. It was this concept that Paul had in mind when he said of Timothy in Philippians 2:22:

> [22] *But you know his **proven character**, that as a son with his father he served with me in the gospel.* (emphasis added)

If we approach the spiritual realm looking only for the instant, we open ourselves up to deception. No one has yet produced instant figs or instant grapes. If anyone were to offer these to us, we would immediately be on our guard. We should likewise be on our guard with ministries that focus only on immediate results that impact our senses.

Jesus made an absolute distinction between the two kinds of trees: A good tree *cannot* bear bad fruit; a bad tree *cannot* bear good fruit. This truth has practical implications. Wherever we encounter bad fruit, we know that its source is a bad tree. We need to identify the bad tree and deal with it.

Jesus concluded with a terrible warning concerning trees that do not produce good fruit: *"Every tree that does not produce good fruit is cut down and thrown into the fire"*

(Matthew 7:19). God demands good fruit. Trees that produce bad fruit and those that produce no fruit come under the same judgment. Their ultimate destiny is the fire of hell.

17

SPIRITUAL GIFTS AND MANIFESTATIONS

Now concerning spiritual gifts, brethren,
I do not want you to be ignorant: you
know that you were Gentiles, carried
away to these dumb idols,
however you were led.
—1 Corinthians 12:1–2

Why did Paul use the word *"dumb"* in the above passage? I do not believe he meant "stupid." What was the point of calling the idols dumb? They never spoke. "Now you are in a spiritual realm," Paul was saying, "where spirits indwell human beings and speak out of them through their vocal organs. Therefore, you need to know whether it is the Holy Spirit that is speaking or a different spirit—that is, an evil spirit, a demon."

Paul then offered a simple, practical test:

³ Therefore I make known to you that no one speaking by the Spirit of God calls Jesus accursed, and no one can say that Jesus is Lord except by the Holy Spirit.
(1 Corinthians 12:3)

Paul had in mind a situation where a spirit has taken up residence within a person and manifests itself through that person. It is not the person's own spirit that we are required to test, but the other spirit that has taken up residence within the person. There is one vital question that we must settle: Is the spirit that is manifesting itself through the person the Holy Spirit from God or is it an evil spirit—a demon?

To apply the test, we must speak directly to the spirit in the person. We must challenge it to reveal its attitude to Jesus: Is Jesus Lord?

If the spirit acknowledges that Jesus is Lord, then it is the Holy Spirit. But if it refuses to acknowledge Jesus as Lord, or even speaks blasphemously against Jesus, then it is an evil spirit—a demon.

I have personally applied this test in many cases. An evil spirit always betrays itself by its reaction. It may seal the mouth of the person and refuse to give any answer. Or it may cause the person to shake his head violently. Or it may speak through the person's mouth negative, blasphemous words against Jesus.

The decisive test is a spirit's attitude toward Jesus. It will either honor Him or deny Him. It will never be neutral.

In his first epistle, John also emphasized the need to test the spirits that we encounter:

> [1] *Beloved, do not believe every spirit, but test the spirits, whether they are of God; because many false prophets have gone out into the world.* (1 John 4:1)

Notice the relationship between a false prophet and a false spirit. A prophet is one who speaks by a spirit that is not his own. If he speaks by the Holy Spirit, he is a true prophet. If he speaks by any other spirit, he is a false prophet. It is the spirit *in* the person that we are testing, not the person's own natural reactions. The decisive issue is the attitude of the spirit toward Jesus.

John continued,

² By this you know the Spirit of God: Every spirit that confesses that Jesus Christ has come in the flesh is of God,

³ and every spirit that does not confess that Jesus Christ has come in the flesh is not of God. (1 John 4:2–3)

Again, the test is primarily the spirit's attitude toward Jesus: Has He come as Christ (Messiah) in the flesh—in a physical body?

⁷ For many deceivers have gone out into the world who do not confess Jesus Christ as coming in the flesh. This is a deceiver and an antichrist.

⁸ Look to yourselves, that we do not lose those things we worked for, but that we may receive a full reward.

⁹ Whoever transgresses [literally, "goes beyond"] and does not abide in the doctrine of Christ does not have God. He who abides in the doctrine of Christ has both the Father and the Son. (2 John 1:7–9)

Notice the essence of the test: Has Jesus the Messiah come in the flesh? If a spirit does not affirm this, it is a deceiver.

What is *"the doctrine of Christ"?* In 1 Corinthians 15:1–5, Paul stated the essential truths that are the foundation of our faith:

¹ Moreover, brethren, I declare to you the gospel which I preached to you, which also you received and in which you stand,

² by which also you are saved, if you hold fast that word which I preached to you— unless you believed in vain.

³ For I delivered to you first of all ["as of the first importance," NIV] that which I also received: that Christ died for our sins according to the Scriptures,

⁴ and that He was buried, and that He rose again the third day according to the Scriptures,

⁵ and that He was seen by Cephas, then by the twelve. (1 Corinthians 15:1–5)

Earlier, in 1 Corinthians 3:11, Paul had stated,

¹¹ For no other foundation can anyone lay than that which is laid, which is Jesus Christ.

When John spoke about someone who "goes beyond" these essential foundational truths, what did he have in mind? It would apply to anyone who adds doctrines beyond these stated by Paul and requires acceptance of them as a condition of salvation. Soulish pride sometimes tempts people into believing some so-called "deeper truth" or some "higher light" granted only to a select few. But thank God that the essential truths of the Gospel are so simple that even a child can understand them. Some people reject the Gospel not because it is too profound but because it is too simple.

As Christians, we are held accountable by God for the way our conduct affects other people. We must be careful not to say or do anything that would be interpreted as condoning or endorsing serious doctrinal error that is being propagated by others—the type of error, that is, that "goes beyond" the simple, basic truths of the Gospel unfolded in the New Testament.

To give a simple, specific example, I believe that the teaching of "Jehovah's Witnesses" clearly *goes beyond* the Gospel unfolded in the New Testament. As a general rule, I would not want to say or do anything that would seem to endorse their errors.

18

WHOM ARE WE NOT RESPONSIBLE TO JUDGE?

In Romans 14 Paul gave examples of people whom we are not required to judge: those who believe they may eat meat, those who believe they should eat only vegetables, those who believe they must observe certain religious days, and those who do not observe any religious days. As long as their observances do not have a negative effect on my life, I am not responsible to judge them. In fact, I am responsible *not* to judge them.

On the other hand, if anything another believer does would influence me to do something unscriptural, then I am responsible to exercise judgment. In other words, the area where I am responsible to judge is my own life and conduct.

JUDGING: WHEN? WHY? HOW?

Another area we are not responsible to judge is other people's children. Sometimes it is very tempting to do that. But again, the same limitation applies: Unless their conduct affects us, we are not to judge them.

Do you know what I have observed? Some of the people who are busy judging other people's children would be better occupied correcting their own.

Another area we are not responsible to judge is Christian groups to which we do not belong. In the New Testament, that situation did not arise because there were no other Christian groups. All Christians belonged to one group. So in a sense it is an unnatural situation.

But let's say you are seriously concerned with the behavior of members of another church. It is not your responsibility to judge them. If you really think the situation needs to be dealt with, go to your shepherd, and he will go to their shepherd. That is the way to handle it: shepherd to shepherd, not sheep to sheep.

19
HOW ARE WE TO JUDGE?

This question is very important. Here are four basic principles of judgment established in Scripture, some or all of which normally apply.

1. Judge with righteous judgment.

2. Judge on the basis of proven fact.

3. The accused has the right to face his accusers.

4. Judge on the basis of at least two and preferably three reliable witnesses.

1. With Righteous Judgment

Jesus warned us:

JUDGING: WHEN? WHY? HOW?

²⁴ Do not judge according to appearance, but judge with righteous judgment.

(John 7:24)

Judging is a serious matter that can have powerful results for good or evil. One way or the other, it can have serious and lasting effects in people's lives. Therefore, we must not indulge in hasty or superficial judgment. We must carefully follow the principles laid down in Scripture.

2. According to the Facts

Second, we must judge on the basis of proven fact. The account given in Genesis 18 really impresses me. The Lord was having a conversation with Abraham, telling him He was on His way to inspect the cities of Sodom and Gomorrah because He had received many bad reports concerning them. (The bad reports, I presume, came from angels.) What impresses me is that the Lord did not merely accept the angels' reports without verifying them for Himself. Listen to what He said:

²⁰ Because the outcry against Sodom and Gomorrah is great, and because their sin is very grave,

²¹ I will go down now and see whether they have done altogether according to the

*outcry against it that has come to Me; and
if not, I will know.* (Genesis 18:20–21)

That amazes me! Even the Lord does not
judge without taking time to see the situation
for Himself. How dare we if God does not?

*[12] If you hear someone in one of your cities,
which the LORD your God gives you to dwell
in, saying:*

*[13] "Corrupt men have gone out from
among you and enticed the inhabitants
of their city, saying, 'Let us go and serve
other gods'"; which you have not known.*
(Deuteronomy 13:12–13)

"If you hear someone...saying." Do you
ever "hear say"? At times, do you even make
judgments only on the basis of hearsay?

The people in this passage were accused
of a terrible sin: turning people away from the
true God to idolatry. How does God expect us
to respond to such a report? I quote from the
King James since it is more vivid than the
other translations:

*[14] Then shall thou **inquire, search out,**
and **ask diligently**. And if it is indeed
true and **certain** that such an abomina-
tion was committed among you,*

¹⁵ you shall surely strike the inhabitants of that city.
(Deuteronomy 13:14–15, emphasis added)

Notice these five safeguards before you act: Inquire, search, ask diligently, see if it is true, and see if it is proven. God ordained for Israel that judgment had to be based on proven facts.

Once just judgment has been decided on, however, then it must be followed up by appropriate action. It frustrates me that Christians are so often passing judgment on other Christians but, after that, they do nothing about it. There is no purpose in judgment if it is not followed by appropriate action. It is unscriptural.

3. Facing the Accusers

The third requirement for judgment is this: The accused has a right to face his accusers and hear the case against him. The worst offenders in this respect are often religious people. In John 7 the Sanhedrin, the Jewish religious council, were discussing Jesus. They had heard a lot of bad reports and were discussing these among themselves. One honest man, Nicodemus, spoke up:

⁵¹ Does our law judge a man before it hears him and knows what he is doing?
(John 7:51)

HOW ARE WE TO JUDGE?

It is not scriptural to judge anybody until you have let that person speak for himself in person.

Some years ago I realized that I was forming opinions of people based on what I had heard, but when I met those people my opinions often changed instantly. I had been going on prejudice and misinformation. So I made a rule of conduct for myself: Whenever possible, I will never form an opinion about somebody until I have met him or her personally. People are so different from what you hear about them!

In Acts 25:15–16 Festus, the Roman procurator, was talking about his dealings with Paul:

> ¹⁵ *About whom the chief priests and the elders of the Jews informed* [misinformed] *me, when I was in Jerusalem, asking for a judgment against him.* (v. 15)

Listen to what this Gentile official told those religious Jews:

> ¹⁶ *It is not the custom of the Romans to deliver any man to destruction before the accused meets the accusers face to face, and has opportunity* [liberty] *to answer for himself concerning the charge against him.* (v. 16)

Festus was upholding to the Jews principles of justice that were established in their own law, but which they were transgressing. Sometimes the secular world is more righteous in its dealings than religious people who are blinded by their prejudices!

4. On the Testimony of Two or Preferably Three Reliable Witnesses

I pointed out earlier that in Matthew 18:16 Jesus Himself affirmed this requirement:

16 That by the mouth of two or three witnesses every word may be established.

In 1 Timothy 5:19 Paul especially emphasized that leaders in the church need the protection of this rule:

19 Do not receive an accusation against an elder except from two or three witnesses.

Why do church leaders especially need this protection? Because Satan is *"the accuser of our brethren"* (Revelation 12:10). Gossip- and scandalmongering are two of the main weapons that Satan uses against men whom God raises up in positions of spiritual leadership. They are also two of the commonest sins among religious people.

* * *

HOW ARE WE TO JUDGE?

At the close of this brief study on judging, we would do well to remind ourselves of one inescapable appointment that awaits us all.

> *10 For we must all appear* [be made manifest, be totally exposed] *before the judgment seat of Christ, that each one may receive the things done in the body, according to what he has done, whether good or bad.*   (2 Corinthians 5:10)

In the next verse, Paul applied this truth to his own life:

> *11 Knowing, therefore, the terror of the Lord, we persuade men; but we are well known* [made manifest, fully exposed] *to God.*
> (v. 11)

Great apostle though he was, Paul was overcome with awe at the prospect of being totally exposed before the judgment seat of Christ. Is there any reason why you or I should find such a prospect less awesome?

APPENDIX 1
HOW TO RECOGNIZE
APOSTLES

In Revelation 2:2 Jesus praised the church at Ephesus: *"You have tested those who say they are apostles and are not, and have found them liars."* Again, in 2 Corinthians 11:13–15, Paul spoke about some who had been ministering among the Corinthians and described them as *"false apostles, deceitful workers, transforming themselves into the apostles of Christ."* Then he commented,

> *14 And no wonder! For Satan himself transforms himself into an angel of light.*
>
> *15 Therefore it is no great thing if his ministers also transform themselves into ministers of righteousness, whose end will be according to their works.* (vv. 14–15)

JUDGING: WHEN? WHY? HOW?

It is clear, therefore, that Jesus holds the church accountable, whenever necessary, to test those who claim to be apostles, and if they do not pass the test, to reject them as deceivers. To reject the false, however, we must first know how to identify the genuine. How, then, can we recognize a true apostle?

First, we must understand what the word *apostle* actually means. The literal meaning of the Greek word for "apostle" is "one sent forth." A person who has not been "sent forth" cannot be an apostle.

In Ephesians 1:22–23 Paul said that God has made Jesus *"head over all things to the church, which is His body."* It is Jesus, therefore, as Head over the church, who sends forth apostles. In 2 Corinthians 3:17, however, Paul said, *"Now the Lord is the Spirit* [that is, the Holy Spirit]."

This statement indicates that Jesus is Lord *over* the church, but that the Holy Spirit is Lord *in* the church. This truth is exemplified in the way that apostles were appointed and sent forth from the Church at Antioch:

> *¹ Now in the church that was at Antioch there were certain prophets and teachers: Barnabas, Simeon who was called Niger,*

Lucius of Cyrene, Manaen who had been brought up with Herod the tetrarch, and Saul [later called Paul].

² As they ministered to the Lord and fasted, the Holy Spirit said, "Now separate to Me Barnabas and Saul for the work to which I have called them."

³ Then, having fasted and prayed, and laid hands on them, they sent them away.

⁴ So, being sent out by the Holy Spirit, they went down to Seleucia, and from there they sailed to Cyprus.   (Acts 13:1–4)

In this transaction, Jesus, as Head over the church, operated through the Holy Spirit—His divine, authoritative, personal representative within the church.

Originally, all of the five men in Acts 13:1 were described as *"prophets and teachers."* After Barnabas and Saul (Paul) had been sent forth, both of them were called *"apostles,"* as in Acts 14:14: *"But when the **apostles** Barnabas and Paul heard this..."* (emphasis added).

It was through being sent forth from Antioch that Barnabas and Paul qualified for the title "apostles."

Later on, Acts 16:1–4 records how a disciple named Timothy was taken in charge by Paul and was sent forth with him as part of his team. In this way, Timothy also qualified for the title "apostle"—"one sent forth." This is confirmed in 1 Thessalonians 1:1 where the epistle opens with readings from three men: Paul, Silvanus (Silas), and Timothy. Further on, in 1 Thessalonians 2:6, Paul, writing on behalf of all three men, said,

> *6 Nor did we seek glory from men, either from you or from others, when we might have made demands as **apostles of Christ.*** (emphasis added)

This verse indicates that Timothy—having been *sent forth* with Paul and Barnabas—was now recognized together with them as an *apostle.*

Paul said,

> *12 Truly the signs of an **apostle** were accomplished among you with all perseverance, in signs and wonders and mighty deeds.*
> (2 Corinthians 12:12, emphasis added)

Obviously, therefore, it was expected that every genuine apostolic ministry would be attested by appropriate supernatural signs.

APPENDIX 1: HOW TO RECOGNIZE APOSTLES

The first attesting sign that Paul mentioned is a distinguishing mark of character: *"all perseverance"* (endurance). When the others are ready to give up, the apostle is the one who holds on in the face of all opposition or discouragement.

> *8 For we do not want you to be ignorant, brethren, of our trouble which came to us in Asia: that we were burdened beyond measure, above strength, so that we despaired even of life.*
>
> *9 Yes, we had the sentence of death in ourselves, that we should not trust in ourselves but in God who raises the dead,*
>
> *10 who delivered us from so great a death, and does deliver us; in whom we trust that He will still deliver us.*
>
> (2 Corinthians 1:8–10)

Then Paul also specified *"signs and wonders and mighty deeds"* (2 Corinthians 2:12). The ministry of an apostle should be attested by significant miracles. An objective reading of the New Testament would indicate that the proclamation of the Gospel should regularly be confirmed by the kind of supernatural attestation described in Hebrews 2:4:

> *4 God also bearing witness both with signs and wonders, with various miracles, and*

gifts of the Holy Spirit, according to His own will.

During the sixty years that I have walked with the Lord, I have had the privilege of getting to know some wonderful servants of His. I do not doubt that some of them qualified for the title "apostle." I think in particular of two men, one from Africa and one from Russia. Their ministries were from time to time attested by dramatic miracles, and they left behind them a trail of local churches. Those are two scriptural marks of an apostle: signs and wonders, and local churches brought to birth.

Supernatural signs by themselves, however, are not necessarily sufficient to attest a ministry as apostolic by New Testament standards. In 2 Thessalonians 2:9 Paul warned that the Antichrist (*"the lawless one"*) will be attested by *"all power, signs, and lying wonders."* Yet, he will be an agent of Satan.

Supernatural signs must be joined with correct doctrine. Acts 2:42 says that those who were baptized on the Day of Pentecost *"continued steadfastly in the apostles' doctrine."* Through this practice they were built up into stable believers.

The entire New Testament is the product of *"the apostles' doctrine."* This fact indicates that the doctrine of a genuine apostle should in all main points harmonize with the total revelation of the New Testament.

Correct doctrine by itself, however, is not enough. It must proceed out of a lifestyle that demonstrates in daily living the truths that we proclaim. In Ephesians 3:4–5 Paul said that the mystery of Christ has been revealed in this age to God's *"**holy** apostles and prophets"* (emphasis added). Revealed truth must always go hand in hand with holiness of life.

In 1 Thessalonians 2:10 Paul spoke on behalf of Silas, Timothy and himself and called the Thessalonians to witness *"how devoutly and justly and blamelessly we behaved ourselves among you who believe."*

The primary fruit of the apostolic ministry is the *local church.* First and foremost, the apostle is the one who knows how to lay the foundation of a local church. Speaking as an apostle to the Corinthians in 1 Corinthians 3:10, Paul said, *"As a wise master builder I have laid the foundation, and another builds on it."*

Beyond that, the apostle also ministers to the various needs of a local church after it has been established. He may be used to bring encouragement, correction, rebuke, and discipline. In relation to the local church the apostle is the *"wise master builder"*—architect. He understands and can supervise every stage in the building process—from laying the foundation to completing the roof.

This brief analysis of the ministry of an apostle leads to two conclusions. First, Christian ministers who lay claim to the title of *"apostle"* should fulfill the qualifications for that ministry that are described in the New Testament. Second, if a local church is approached by ministers laying claim to the title of apostles, the leaders of the church are responsible to check their claim by the standards of the New Testament.

APPENDIX 2
TRUE AND FALSE
PROPHETS

When we enter into the fullness of the Christian life, as depicted in the New Testament, we find ourselves projected out of the natural and into a supernatural level of living. With the supernatural, we enter into a realm of greatly increased potential, but also of new and unfamiliar dangers.

We may illustrate this truth by a simple example from electricity. The higher the voltage of the current that runs through a wire, the more powerful the insulation that protects the wire needs to be. So it is also in the spiritual realm. The further we move into the realm of the supernatural, the more urgent our need of the spiritual "insulation" that God has provided for us.

JUDGING: WHEN? WHY? HOW?

The "insulation" that I have in mind consists of studying and carefully applying the various safeguards that God has provided in Scripture to keep the gift and ministry of a prophet in line with His Holy Word.

Satan's primary weapon against humanity has always been *deception.* It was by deception that he ensnared Adam and Eve in the beginning of human history. In the last book of the Bible, the climax of prophecy and of history, he is identified as *"that serpent of old, called the Devil and Satan, who **deceives** the whole world"* (Revelation 12:9, emphasis added).

God has had His prophets on the earth in all ages. The first prophecy recorded in Scripture was given by Enoch in the seventh generation from Adam:

14 Behold, the Lord comes with ten thousands of His saints,

15 to execute judgment on all. (Jude 14–15)

Abraham, the father of God's people on earth, was a prophet. The Lord told Abimelech concerning him, *"He is a prophet, and he will pray for you and you shall live"* (Genesis 20:7).

APPENDIX 2: TRUE AND FALSE PROPHETS

In the New Covenant, in Ephesians 4:11, *"prophets"* are one of the five main ministries that Jesus has provided for the upbuilding of His body, the church.

Under the Law of Moses, God gave specific directions to His people as to how to distinguish between true and false prophets. In Deuteronomy 13:1–5 the Lord warned that a prophet may give some supernatural sign, which actually comes to pass, and yet he may be a false prophet:

> *¹ If there arises among you a prophet or a dreamer of dreams, and he gives you a sign or a wonder,*
>
> *² and the sign or the wonder comes to pass, of which he spoke to you, saying, "Let us go after other gods"; which you have not known; "and let us serve them,"*
>
> *³ you shall not listen to the words of that prophet or that dreamer of dreams, for the LORD your God is testing you to know whether you love the LORD your God with all your heart and with all your soul.*
>
> *⁴ You shall walk after the LORD your God and fear Him, and keep His commandments and obey His voice, and you shall serve Him and hold fast to Him.*

> *⁵ But that prophet or that dreamer of dreams shall be put to death, because he has spoken in order to turn you away from the LORD your God, who brought you out of the land of Egypt and redeemed you from the house of bondage, to entice you from the way in which the LORD your God commanded you to walk. So you shall put away the evil from your midst.*

This warning is urgently needed today. Some of God's people are so enamored of the supernatural that they are ready to receive anyone who demonstrates supernatural power or knowledge as necessarily being a true servant of God. But the passage quoted above indicates that this attitude is unscriptural and dangerous.

In the seventh and eighth chapters of Exodus, the magicians of Egypt could duplicate the first three supernatural signs performed by Moses and Aaron. They could turn their rods into serpents; they could turn water into blood; they could call swarms of frogs out of the river. Yet those magicians were servants of Satan, and their supernatural power came from Satan.

In Deuteronomy 13:3 Moses gave one reason why God may at times permit us to be

confronted by prophets who perform supernatural signs by a power that is not from
God:

> ³ **For the L**ORD **your God is testing you**
> *to know whether you love the L*ORD *your*
> *God with all your heart and with all your*
> *soul.*
>   (Deuteronomy 13:3, emphasis added)

Our only absolute and unfailing protection
from deception is wholehearted love for the
Lord and uncompromising respect and obedience to His Word contained in the Scriptures.

In all dispensations, God permits our love
for Him to be tested. In Revelation 3:18 Jesus
spoke to the church at Laodicea,

> ¹⁸ *I counsel you to buy from Me gold refined*
> *in the fire.*

Refined gold is love that has stood the test
of obedience. It is never cheap!

In Deuteronomy 18:20–22 Moses gave a
further way to identify a false prophet:

> ²⁰ *But the prophet who presumes to speak*
> *a word in My name, which I have not com-*
> *manded him to speak, or who speaks in*
> *the name of other gods, that prophet shall*
> *die.*

²¹ And if you say in your heart, "How shall we know the word which the LORD has not spoken?";

²² when a prophet speaks in the name of the LORD, if the thing does not happen or come to pass, that is the thing which the LORD has not spoken; the prophet has spoken it presumptuously; you shall not be afraid of him.

To get the full picture we need to combine the two passages that show us how to identify a false prophet: Deuteronomy 13:1–5 and Deuteronomy 18:20–22.

The first passage warns against a prophet who gives a supernatural sign that is fulfilled, but at the same time teaches disobedience or disloyalty towards the Lord. The second passage warns that a prophet who makes some supernatural prediction that is not fulfilled is a false prophet.

By induction we arrive at the following conclusion: A true prophet is one who gives a supernatural sign or makes a prediction that is fulfilled, but who also teaches loyalty and obedience to the Lord and to His Word.

If a professing Christian gives a supernatural sign or a prophetic prediction that is not fulfilled, he or she should take the following steps:

(1) Publicly acknowledge that the sign or the prediction was false.

(2) Ask forgiveness of all those who were deceived.

(3) If people who were deceived suffered loss or damage, do everything possible to make amends.

During the sixty years that I have been walking with the Lord I can recall at least half a dozen situations in which—in the name of the Lord—a man or a woman gave a supernatural sign or made a predictive prophecy that was never fulfilled. I can recall only two of those persons who publicly acknowledged their sin and asked forgiveness of those who had been deceived.

In the New Testament church God has ordained that the exercise of the gift of prophecy should be publicly submitted to testing:

> [29] Let two or three prophets speak, and let the others judge.   (1 Corinthians 14:29)

It is unscriptural to permit the exercise of the gift of prophecy in public unless opportunity is given for it to be subjected to testing.

JUDGING: WHEN? WHY? HOW?

I can recall a Sunday morning when I found myself on the platform of a church where I was a regularly invited speaker. At one point a man near the back stood up and in a loud, harsh voice gave forth a prophecy that poured condemnation on all the sins and shortcomings of the people present.

As the man was speaking, I was watching some college students who were sitting in a group near the front. The longer the man went on "prophesying," the more clearly their faces registered skepticism and disgust. "If no one challenges that man," I said to myself, "those intelligent, impressionable young people will conclude that we—their elders—accept what that man is saying as a genuine manifestation of the Holy Spirit, and they will lose all confidence in the kind of Christianity that we profess."

When the man had come to the end of his "prophecy," I stood up and addressed the congregation: "The New Testament teaches that when anyone prophesies, the others present should judge what he has been saying. It also says that a person who prophesies speaks edification, exhortation, and comfort. (See 1 Corinthians 14:3.) In everything that our brother has been saying, I have heard nothing that I would describe as edification, exhortation, or comfort—only criticism and condemnation. For my part, I do not accept it as a genuine prophecy.

"The New Testament also says, *'Let the others judge'* (1 Corinthians 14:29). I invite others here to give their judgment."

There were a few moments of silence. Then—one after another—three men who were respected in the congregation stood up and gave their judgment. Each of them endorsed what I had said.

The dark cloud that had followed the man's fake prophecy was dispelled. More important still, the faces of the college students relaxed. Their elders were not so easily fooled, after all.

Prophecy is a precious gift that Jesus has provided for the upbuilding of the church. Rightly exercised, it is a channel of great blessing—of edification, exhortation and comfort. But its counterfeit—false prophecy—can be a satanic tool used for the destruction of God's people. I can recall instances where false prophecy has been an instrument in the destruction of an individual, a family, and even a whole congregation.

JUDGING: WHEN? WHY? HOW?

This places an obligation upon all who are leaders of God's people to faithfully and diligently apply the safeguards that God has provided in Scripture.

ANOTHER POWERFUL BOOK
from Whitaker House

Spiritual Warfare
Derek Prince

Derek Prince explains the battle that's happening now between the forces of God and the forces of evil. Choose to be prepared by learning the enemy's strategies so you can effectively block his attack. We have God on our side and nothing will keep us from victory.

ISBN: 0-88368-670-8
Trade
144 pages

ANOTHER POWERFUL *B*OOK
from Whitaker House

God's Remedy for Rejection
Derek Prince

Rejection is a common experience that can cause permanent spiritual wounds, whether we are aware of them or not. Derek Prince shows how God can bring healing to your wounds and can bring you into acceptance with Himself and the family of God. Discover how you can leave the effects of rejection behind permanently.

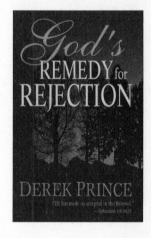

ISBN: 0-88368-483-7
Pocket
112 pages